Original title:
Lace in the Moonlight

Copyright © 2025 Creative Arts Management OÜ
All rights reserved.

Author: Alec Davenport
ISBN HARDBACK: 978-1-80586-083-9
ISBN PAPERBACK: 978-1-80586-555-1

A Silhouette in Starlit Patterns

In the night, shadows creep,
Like a cat with secrets to keep.
Twinkling stars, a clumsy dance,
Swirling patterns in a dream-like trance.

Beneath the glow, a mischief's grin,
As frogs in tuxedos break out in spin.
Socks on hands and hats askew,
Twilight giggles at all we do.

Ethereal Patterns in the Moonshadow

Moonbeams play on the garden wall,
A rabbit wearing shoes starts to crawl.
With each hop and silly stride,
He quips and quirks, like he's filled with pride.

The owls hoot in bewildered cheer,
As shadows dance, there's no need for fear.
A picnic blanket, a juggling act,
Chasing fireflies, oh, what a fact!

Shimmering Dreams in Celestial Silk

Stars twinkle like a thousand eyes,
As garden gnomes plot their surprise.
Chasing comets, with laughter so bright,
They tumble and giggle, what a sight!

With cupcakes floating on starry trails,
We dine on smiles and moonlit tales.
Dogs in top hats, grinning with glee,
In the silk of dreams, wild and free.

Whispered Threads of Twilight

Twilight weaves its cozy thread,
As squirrels in bowties dance overhead.
With each twirl, they spin their trick,
While chasing nuts that vanish quick.

A hedgehog juggling acorns round,
In this wild concert, laughter's found.
Clouds burst forth with pops and cheers,
As twilight whispers in our ears.

Night's Fragile Adornment

Beneath the stars, a dance takes flight,
A cat in shoes, oh what a sight!
He trips on dreams, with grace so odd,
While chasing shadows, he gives a nod.

A firefly caught in a tangle of twine,
Thinks it's a ride on a roller coaster line.
With giggles and sparks, they lose the race,
The moon just chuckles, it knows their pace.

Twilight Looms of Imagination

As dusk paints whispers, ideas will bloom,
A hamster in goggles zooms round the room.
He finds a new world behind the fridge,
Where pickles are kings and lettuce is a bridge.

The clouds float by, a cotton candy dream,
Where squirrels play chess, it's quite the theme.
They wager acorns and giggle with cheer,
While the night wraps laughter, it holds them near.

Mystical Weavings of the Night

The owl wears glasses, perched on a tree,
Reading the tales of bees' poetry.
He flips through pages of buzzing delight,
As the moon laughs softly, embracing the night.

A rabbit with boots hops onto the scene,
In search of the stars, dressed up like a queen.
With each little bounce, it snags a few rays,
While crickets join in for a symphonic phase.

Dark Fabrics of Fantasia

In the fabric of night, a wizard appears,
With socks on his hands and giggles as cheers.
He stirs up the dreams in a bubbling pot,
Adjusts his big hat, oh what a plot!

A raccoon in pajamas peers from a bush,
With marshmallow wishes, he starts with a hush.
They twirl and they spin in a waltz of delight,
As starlight and laughter take flight through the night.

Starlit Tapestry of Secrets

Under stars, a tangled mess,
Whispers laugh, they do confess.
A cat in boots tries to impress,
While mice twirl, they don't digress.

Moonlit pranks, they play a tune,
Bouncing rabbits, over the dune.
While owls hoot a silly boon,
The night is giggles, none too soon.

Ethereal Dances Under the Night Sky

Fairies jig on mushrooms bright,
Wings flutter, oh what a sight!
Goblins join, with glee and fright,
Twirling wildly, all in flight.

Stars wink down, a cosmic jest,
While crickets chirp, they do their best.
A dance-off starts, you're unimpressed,
But who knew night could be so blessed?

Patterns of a Celestial Veil

With cosmic threads, the night is spun,
Joking stars that laugh and run.
Each twinkle hides a bit of fun,
Their brilliance shines, a gleeful pun.

The moon rolls over, causing a ruck,
As comets chase in silly luck.
Asteroids bounce, a cosmic chuck,
The universe laughs, it's all in luck.

Silken Echoes of the Night

Whispers echo, the night's café,
Cats in tuxes now start to sway.
With jokes on stars, they play all day,
Dodging meteors on their way.

Crickets croon, a smooth serenade,
While moonbeams join, a prancing parade.
In shadows, laughter's softly made,
With giggles blowing like the glade.

Veils of Desire Under Starry Skies

Twinkling lights up above,
Dancing like socks in a dryer,
Whispers of secrets in love,
Oh, what a glorious liar!

A cat in a hat prances proud,
With dreams that would tickle a mouse,
The stars nodding laughter so loud,
As shadows do jig on a douse.

A cupcake in hand takes a spin,
While moonbeams tie knots in my hair,
Balloons float and start their own kin,
Adventures, they bubble with flair!

Frogs croak the notes of a tune,
Scooters ride on clouds made of cream,
Chasing the glow of the moon,
Life's just one big fluffy dream!

The Night's Silken Embrace.

Beneath a blanket of winks,
The sky wears a sparkling grin,
Daisies play hide-and-seek,
With pixies, they bounce and spin.

A toaster hums songs in the night,
While shadows waltz in the breeze,
Laughter erupts from the light,
As crickets wear shoes with ease.

The stars tell tales of their past,
Some silly, some grand, and some bright,
As time twirls around us so fast,
In this fabric, we twine with delight.

Night whispers jokes with a grin,
While dreams peek through eyelids wide,
The silly sights swirl and spin,
As whims make it hard to decide!

Whispers of Night's Embrace

The owl hoots with a wisecrack,
As the moon takes a spin on the lawn,
With giggles that bounce off the track,
And shadows that jump like a fawn.

Stars wink like kids in a prank,
Playing hide-and-seek from afar,
Each twinkle, a chuckle, a yank,
While fireflies dance in a jar.

The breeze blows a secret so sweet,
It tickles the toes of the grass,
As mischief and fun intercede,
In this curious tapestry, we pass.

Imaginations soar with a cheer,
Silly dreams dash through the night,
In whispers and giggles sincere,
The world glimmers, all feels just right!

Gossamer Dreams Unfold

In shadows where giggles imply,
The night unfolds with a tease,
With critters in hats passing by,
And whispers that bounce on the breeze.

The stars dress up in their best,
Sparkling with rubies and jade,
As the moon plays games with the rest,
In a caper that never will fade.

A squirrel tightrope walks on a line,
While dreams wear a crown made of fluff,
Caught in a wink, drifting divine,
Where laughter alone is enough.

The night's a parade full of jest,
With mischief, like sprinkles on cake,
In this fabric, we all feel blessed,
As soft shadows pirouette and shake!

Celestial Draperies

Stars hang like curtains,
In a sky that's delightfully tight.
The moon winks with humor,
Casting shadows that giggle at night.

Clouds puff like cotton,
Waltzing in a cosmic dance.
They bump into the starlight,
And fall backward in a prance.

The night's a feathery creature,
Tickling the world's dark nooks.
With each twinkle and shimmer,
Even the owls crack jokes in their books.

So gather with the starlings,
For a night of giggly cheer.
In fabrics of the firmament,
There's fun enough to last all year.

Nocturnal Tapestry

The night wears a silly scarf,
Comically tangled in the breeze.
Moonbeams play hopscotch above,
As crickets hum their melodies.

Bats in their tiny tuxedos,
Zooming like they own the place.
They flip and spin in laughter,
Chasing the stars in a race.

A wise old owl, quite dapper,
Tells jokes in a feathery tone.
While shadows dance with giggles,
In this grand, vast twilight zone.

Each stitch of night a wonder,
Woven with a wink and glee.
Come laugh with the constellations,
Under a sky so carefree.

Moonlit Elegance

Moonlight sparkles like sequins,
Draped on a cheeky face.
The night twirls in a gown,
Proudly holding the starry lace.

Breezes whisper silly tales,
Of mermaids trying to fly.
While comets slide in giggles,
Leaving trails that wink goodbye.

A party of – wait, is that a raccoon?
Dancing under the glowing beams.
It's all so wonderfully goofy,
Even the shadows have dreams.

In this fancy gala of mischief,
Where every twinkle's a jest,
The universe joins the fun,
In a whimsical, moonlit fest.

Filigree of the Dark

The night's a jester, all dressed up,
In layers of sparkly threads.
It tickles the sleeping rooftops,
As stars play hop on beds.

With a chuckle and a twinkle,
The moon guides the chaos anew.
Each shadow boasts a punchline,
As laughter spills, a cosmic view.

From rooftops to the valleys,
The echoes of humor throng.
In the quilt of the darkened sky,
Where the night sings its funny song.

So join this merry gathering,
Beneath the winks of cosmic art.
In this playful filigree,
Let the night tickle your heart.

Glimmers of Twilight's Whisper

In the night, squirrels dance and prance,
Hiding nuts in their silly stance.
A cat yawns wide, a real surprise,
Wearing moonlight as his disguise.

The stars wink down with funny cheer,
Let's drink lemonade without fear!
Goats in pajamas leap so high,
Don't ask me why, just let it fly!

Frogs wear crowns with great delight,
Holding court on a lily's height.
They croak sweet songs, all off the beat,
Wiggling their toes to feel the heat.

Dreams tumble in like a playful breeze,
With giggly shadows among the trees.
As moonbeams laugh, we weave our fun,
In twilight's charm, our joy has begun.

Celestial Stitches in the Dark

Stars sew stories with shiny threads,
Telling tales of mischievous beds.
Rabbits in bowties hop and sway,
While owls study comic books all day.

The moon wears glasses, a sight to see,
Making faces with glee and esprit.
Pigeon post from the sky above,
Delivers giggles, wrapped in love.

Clouds play tag while zephyrs chase,
Tickling the leaves, a cheeky grace.
A hedgehog spins at the party's side,
Cactus in hat, he beams with pride.

With every twinkle, laughter blooms,
Shadows pirouette in silly rooms.
In darkness stitched, we weave our night,
With threads of laughter, what a sight!

Enchanted Threads of a Starry Veil

Underneath a blanket of twinkling joy,
Silly thoughts as bright as a toy.
A bear with cupcakes dreams away,
While frogs wear shoes, they prance and sway.

Candles flicker, they sing and hum,
While squirrels tap dance to a drumming thrum.
Raccoons in the pantry, snack in hand,
Count their treasures in a merry band.

Balloons a-float, they tickle the air,
Sprinkling laughter everywhere.
A moonlit pie, oh what a treat,
A slice of giggles, can't be beat!

As whispers giggle in the starry sea,
Let's sew our dreams with glee, just we!
With every stitch, we'll craft our way,
Through silly nights, let fun at play!

Gossamer Hues of the Dreamscape

In a world where jellybeans bounce,
And gummy bears dance, let's announce!
Under starlit skies, we'll spin and glide,
On candy clouds, let's take a ride.

With faeries giggling, on firefly light,
Exploring the wonders of the soft night.
A parrot in shades, he shows off flair,
While turtles in sneakers race without care.

Giggling dolphins leap from the deep,
Tickling the stars as they softly creep.
In whispers, magic colors bloom,
Turning wild dreams into a room.

Let's drink our joy like fizzy pop,
And dance with shadows till we drop.
In hues of mischief, let's play our part,
With laughter woven into every heart.

Glowing Through the Gloom

In the dark with a twinkle, quite tight,
A cat in a hat makes a silly sight.
With socks on his paws, he prances around,
Chasing shadows and giggles, oh what a sound.

A moonbeam slips in, the light has a dance,
A weasel in spectacles takes a chance.
He trips in the grass where the daisies grow,
With a hop and a skip, his antics steal the show.

The owl with a wink wears a bowtie too bright,
He hoots in a rhythm, oh what a delight.
Toadstools are dancing, a warty old crew,
As the night drifts on by, they put on a review.

The starry confetti floats down from above,
A few stumbles, a tumble, but all's full of love.
In the glow of the night, all worries take flight,
With laughter like bubbles, we're joyous and light.

Twilight's Soft Embrace

Underneath a sky of spun candy fluff,
A squirrel with a cape thinks he's quite tough.
He leaps from a branch, his landing a mess,
With a thud and a fumble, he's anyone's guess.

A rabbit in slippers hops up for the show,
While giggling at clouds that are starting to glow.
He brings out some popcorn and sprinkles it right,
Telling tales of the day and the mischief at night.

An audience forms, with a blink and a cheer,
A frog wearing glasses croaks loud and clear.
He sings silly songs to the crickets' delight,
With a rhythm that wiggles, oh, this feels just right!

When stars start to twinkle, the mayhem begins,
As fireflies join in with their flashing grins.
Beneath twilight's blanket, the laughter expands,
Creating a party that night understands.

Night's Fabric of Wonders

A raccoon in pearls has a delightful plan,
She's hosting a gala with a tiny dance band.
The spoons form a circle, the cheese beads align,
As the night comes alive with a sparkly shine.

A hedgehog in slippers struts onto the floor,
With a wiggle and jiggle, he shimmies for sure.
He twirls and he spins, his quills all askew,
But the band plays on, and the fun's never through.

The moon grins wide at the playful parade,
While shadows join in, uninvited charade.
A chorus of giggles, from up in the trees,
Makes the night silly, like a summer breeze.

So gather your friends, let the antics ignite,
In this fabric of wonders, we giggle with delight.
As stars watch in awe, they twinkle with glee,
This fabric we weave, is all about whimsy!

Moon's Hidden Embellishments

The moon wears a dress, sparkly and bright,
With frills made of clouds, oh what a sight!
Is that a star stuck beneath her hem,
Or just a bug with a questionable whim?

Crickets chirp secrets to the gentle breeze,
As fireflies giggle, swaying with ease.
In shadows they dance, a mischievous crew,
Making mischief beneath skies of blue.

Glistening Folds of Night

Underneath the silver, the world gets a twist,
Even owls can't help but flap and insist!
A raccoon in a tuxedo struts by with flair,
While moonbeams giggle at mischief laid bare.

The flowers whisper jokes to giggling trees,
Telling tales of dandelion bees.
Each rustle a chuckle, each shimmer a tease,
As nighttime takes hold, it's aiming to please.

Melodies of Shadows

Shadows hold hands in a playful array,
Chasing the sun on its final foray.
A cat with a swagger leaps high, and then pause,
Looking for trouble with no real cause.

The moon croons softly a tune from afar,
While marshmallows tumble in dreams like stars.
Chirps turn to giggles, soft sighs turn to cheer,
As nocturnal beings conspire with cheer.

The Night's Tender Embrace

In the arms of twilight, the giggles abound,
Squirrels are playing hide-and-seek on the ground.
The stars roll their eyes, can you believe,
What a ruckus this night can achieve?

Moonlight wrinkles the grass like a silly old dog,
As frogs serenade without any fog.
With a waltz on the breeze and a pies crusted grin,
The night's simple joy wraps everyone in.

Enchanted Nightfall

A raccoon wore a frilly dress,
Under the glow, he made quite a mess.
Dancing with shadows, a sight to behold,
Wobbling around like a marionette old.

The owls hooted, they couldn't quite stare,
As the moon gave a wink, full of playful flair.
The wind teased the trees, with a giggle and spin,
While squirrels danced bravely, in their squirrelly skin.

Stars were twinkling, demanding a jest,
As frogs croaked their tales, never second-best.
A joyous parade, under nights so absurd,
Where laughter was king, and pranks were the word.

With feathers and sparkles all over the grass,
The creatures looked chic, they were dressed to impress.
Under enchanted nightfall, the world spun around,
In a tapestry woven with giggles profound.

The Fabric of Twilight

In the fading light, a llama took flight,
Sporting a bonnet, what a silly sight!
Chasing the fireflies, in a whimsical race,
With a laugh and a leap, he twirled through the space.

A hedgehog in heels, oh what a display,
Tiptoeing gracefully, in his own quirky way.
He tripped on the poppies, did a little spin,
And laughed at the garden, inviting in sin.

Moonbeams that giggled, painted the ground,
As bunnies wore tutus, hopping around.
The scene was so silly, it made the stars cheer,
In the fabric of twilight, there's nothing to fear.

As shadows grew long, and laughter took flight,
The world shifted gears, into jolly delight.
Patches of whimsy stitched into the night,
Twilight stitched laughter, in stitches so bright.

Glimmers Beneath the Stars

A cat in a top hat, so dapper and fine,
Sipped on some moonlight, oh how divine!
He tipped it to mice, who were dancing around,
In little tuxedos, they made silly sounds.

Beneath the bright stars, a party took flight,
With cupcakes and sprinkles, a sugary night.
Dancing on clouds, with twinkling delight,
The critters all cheered, "Goodbye to sunlight!"

A raccoon was juggling, with style and flair,
Bowling a snicker, his act to ensnare.
The stars giggled back, shared in the fun,
Under a blanket of laughter, for everyone.

Glimmers so silly, in patterns and twists,
As shadows played tag, you wouldn't want to miss.
With joy in the air, they danced till the dawn,
A festival of fun, until the night's gone.

Whispered Secrets in Silk

An octopus waltzed, with ribbons galore,
In a ballroom of bubbles, he danced on the floor.
His moves were so funny, they sparked quite a cheer,
As fish joined the rhythm, with giggles sincere.

Seahorses twirled, in their best flowing gowns,
Mimicking starfish, in whimsical crowns.
Under waves whispering secrets of silk,
The night echoed laughter, smoother than milk.

With every deep current, a pool of delight,
The creatures converged, into the soft night.
Their giggles cascaded, like pearls from the sea,
Whispered secrets in silk, forever carefree.

As lanterns of jellyfish glowed bright overhead,
The party continued, they danced instead.
With tentacles spinning, and tails all a-flap,
Whispers of silk wrapped them in a laugh.

The Night's Silvery Kiss

The stars wear gowns of twinkling gold,
As owls dance lightly, bold and old.
A cat with a hat meows a tune,
While shadows play a game with the moon.

The breeze brings laughter, soft and bright,
Silly whispers tickle the night.
A rabbit hops in polka-dot shoes,
Mixing cocktails of stars with grape juice!

Twirling through dreams on invisible strings,
Chasing the laughter that midnight brings.
With every giggle, the night responds,
In this wacky world, our dream life bonds.

Shimmering echoes of playful glee,
As the moon takes a sip of tea.
With every chuckle, the stars burst wide,
In this funny dance, we all glide.

Moonbeams Between the Folds

Draped in fabric of shimmering light,
Creatures convene for a comical night.
A hedgehog in sneakers does a quick step,
While a frog on a drum plays a real prep.

Twirling about in a skirt made of dreams,
Balloons float high, or so it seems.
The stars giggle as they sway,
While crickets hold a rock 'n' roll play.

With every twirl, they spin and they frolic,
Tickling the air with laughter so brolic.
Puppets dance as the moon pulls strings,
In this ruckus, we've all found wings.

So we'll dance till dawn with wild delight,
In the folds of magic where shadows ignite.
With a wink and a nod, we all share a laugh,
In this joyous dance, we'll find a new path.

Weaving Dreams in the Silence

Silence whispers in playful tones,
As fireflies begin their prancing zones.
A raccoon in shades takes a stroll,
While knitting a scarf with an old donut roll.

The clouds roll by in a fluffy parade,
Holding secrets in dreams they've made.
Each stitch is a chuckle, each purl a cheer,
In this cozy corner where silliness is dear.

An old tortoise with a top hat arrives,
Teaching the stars how to do high-fives.
With each giggle, the night's warmth creep,
As everyone gathers, it's time for sleep.

So let's weave our dreams with laughter so bright,
In the quiet of night, we'll ignite insight.
With every twinkle, we'll find our muse,
In this magical silence, we'll never lose.

Fleeting Moments of Night

Moments flutter like moths in flight,
Tickling our toes with pure delight.
A squirrel juggles acorns with flair,
While owls hoot a rhythm, oh so rare.

The moon dims down in a playful haze,
As shadows engage in a silly maze.
A dog in pajamas starts to break dance,
As the night brims over with whimsical chance.

With giggles echoing throughout the trees,
Pixies fly low on a wobbly breeze.
Silly songs spill from the heart of the night,
As every giggle commands the moon's light.

So let's celebrate these fleeting calls,
While laughter bounces off backyard walls.
In each shared moment, let's find our way,
To a funny tale where we'll forever stay.

Threads of the Nightingale

In shadows where hilarity plays,
Birds wear wigs, and squirrels sway.
Moonbeam parties spin round and round,
As laughter echoes from the ground.

Twirling cats in polka dot suits,
Chase chipmunks donning funny boots.
With every chuckle, stars align,
While owls hoot jokes—oh, how divine!

Giggling flowers dance in delight,
Giving chase to the butterflies' flight.
While fireflies flash their comedy show,
The night dons a smile, all aglow!

Beneath a blanket stitched with glee,
Frogs perform in harmony.
The nightingale, with feathers so spry,
Turns jokes into melodies on high.

Dark Silhouettes of Grace

In the twilight, shadows prance,
As penguins start a graceful dance.
With twirls and spins, they steal the show,
While crickets cheer and applaud in row.

A raccoon wearing a top hat bright,
Tells jokes to raccoons, sparks delight.
The moon winks, with a subtle grin,
As the night grows silly, let the fun begin!

Bats hang upside down, giggling so low,
While rabbits hop to a silly show.
In dark silhouettes, laughter takes flight,
Transforming the stars into humorous light.

With every gust of the cool night breeze,
The giggles weave through the autumn leaves.
Here's to a night of whimsy and cheer,
In a world where laughter is always near!

Whispering Waves of Evening

The tides giggle in moonlit play,
As jellyfish don their flapper sway.
Seashells gossip in gentle waves,
While sea otters prance, oh how they behave!

Mermaids strut like they own the shore,
Telling tales of mischief and more.
With bubbles popping like champagne corks,
The ocean's pulses mimic exuberant quirks.

A crab in a bowtie walks with flair,
While dolphins leap, flashing a smile rare.
The whispering waves call out in jest,
As fish in bright colors perform their best.

Back on land, stars waltz with delight,
Joining in with the whimsical night.
Laughter ripples, a joyful refrain,
In the symphony where the silly remains.

Twilight's Subtle Intricacies

In the dusk, the shadows conspire,
As lightning bugs play in a conga line higher.
The whispers of evening, a giggly affair,
While the stars peek through, with a twinkling stare.

A bear on a unicycle rolls with flair,
As the owls shriek, "Did you see that pair?"
With mismatched socks and colorful hats,
The twilight troupe performs with laughs and spats.

A parade of frogs in sunglasses bright,
Jump from lily pads, oh what a sight!
Dancing beneath the sky's soft embrace,
In twilight's intricacies, giggles we trace.

The night collects whispers, tales in the air,
As creatures share secrets, weaving their hair.
With every chuckle, the evening ignites,
In a charming ballet of whimsical nights.

A Glimpse of Moonlit Threads

Stars are laughing in the sky,
While I dance, oh me, oh my.
A hiccup here, a twirl goes wrong,
My socks are tangled, what a song!

Lunchtime giggles fill the air,
With noodles stuck in my wild hair.
The moon peeks down, it's quite a sight,
As I moonwalk in pajamas tight.

What if the moon joined the spree?
Would it twirl and trip like me?
I picture it with a cap and bowl,
Sipping lemonade, oh what a goal!

So when night falls, and shadows play,
I'll cha-cha in my toothy way.
With every giggle, my spirits rise,
In this dance of clumsy, moonlit skies.

Twilight's Gentle Touch

Twilight whispers secrets sweet,
As I stomp my clumsy feet.
Mice are chuckling, tails entwined,
In this charming night, I find.

A serenade of frogs tonight,
They croak a tune, oh what a fright!
I trip on shadows, spill my drink,
The stars all wink, they start to blink.

With each misstep, I feel so bold,
The moon cracks up, or so I'm told.
Dancing socks, oh what a show,
As twilight paints my moves in glow.

So let's embrace the goofy scene,
In shimmered light, I'll feel like queen.
For night's soft touch brings whimsy fair,
A nightly jest in frolic's air.

A Kiss from the Evening Star

An evening star winks with glee,
Just tripped on air, oh look at me!
Unruly hair, a timeless mess,
But who can care? I must confess.

The fireflies join my crazy dance,
What a sight to see them prance!
I laugh at shadows on my feet,
The moon is busy with its treat.

I'll spin and twirl like never before,
While crickets play an encore score.
Each twinkling star, a giggling mate,
In this party, I celebrate!

So come along, you twinkle bright,
Let's make this a hilarious night!
With funny moves and boisterous cheer,
The evening star will disappear.

Flickers of Silk and Shadow

In shades of shadows, I pirouette,
With giggles, I can't quite forget.
The curtains sway, can they believe,
That I can leap and hardly grieve?

The night has quirks, a funny mood,
With rhymes and riddles, laughter brewed.
Each flicker brings a quirky grin,
As twinkling dreams leap from within.

The breeze is tickling my silly toes,
While shadows draft the funny prose.
I juggle wishes, round and round,
In this gloaming, laughter's found.

So here's to nights of carefree fun,
With every stomp, I'm never done!
Through silk and shadows, I will glide,
In a dance where silly dreams abide.

Shimmering Patterns of Rest

The stars wear funny hats at night,
With giggles caught in silver lights.
They dance upon the sleepy trees,
While moonbeams peek and fold their knees.

A cat in boots, he struts with flair,
And holds a moonlit masquerade pair.
He twirls with twinkling, shining white,
And winks at dreams that take to flight.

The shadows chuckle, soft and sly,
As owls hoot jokes beneath the sky.
Each breeze is filled with little tales,
Of troubadours on shooting gales.

With each new plan the night unveils,
A little moonlit ship sets sails.
To sail on laughter's gentle seas,
Where joy's the anchor, and dance the breeze.

Twilight's Whispering Weave

In twilight's grip, the frogs hold court,
With tiny crowns, their jests come short.
They ribbit tunes of froggy cheer,
While colors swirl, with giggles clear.

The bats wear glasses, quite absurd,
Debating quirks of flying birds.
While chubby fireflies waltz around,
In sparkly skirts, they twirl and bound.

The grass sings softly 'neath their feet,
Composing sonnets, oh-so-sweet.
A symphony of silly sounds,
As mischief dances all around.

With a wink and nod, the night unfolds,
In lacey secrets, laughter molds.
For every chuckle, there's a thrill,
In twilight's weave, our hearts stand still.

The Night's Gilded Graces

Beneath the glee of shining spheres,
The night spins tales to tease our ears.
With hints of gold and playful schemes,
It tickles dreams and laughs in beams.

An owl in slippers sips his tea,
While squirrels jest at his decree.
Each leaf, a witness, sways in glee,
As shadows clap, a wild spree.

The moon throws kisses, soft and sly,
On giggly ghosts that drift and fly.
They whisper jokes and giggles bright,
In the cozy hush of starry night.

Oh, the night wears crowns of twinkling grace,
With silly antics in every space.
As we embrace the soft delight,
The gilded charms of humor's light.

Mysteries in Velvet Darkness

In shadows deep, where secrets flit,
The night reveals its quirky wit.
With velvet drapes that twist and sway,
The mysteries laugh and play all day.

A rabbit dons a cloak of stars,
Reciting jokes from ancient bars.
He hops between the Christmast trees,
And shares bizarre, enchanting tease.

The moon plays hide and seek with glee,
While owls snicker at the spree.
With every riddle wrapped in night,
The velvet whispers tease our sight.

So let us dance 'neath hidden charms,
With giggles soft and open arms.
For in this darkness, laughter's glow,
Reveals the fun we're yet to know.

Ethereal Stitches of Time

When shadows play with mischief's glee,
The stars begin a ragged spree.
A thread unwinds in twinkling grace,
As giggles fill the cosmic space.

A needle darts through dreams so bright,
Each stitch a prank in playful flight.
The fabric bends, the colors blend,
And time itself just loves to bend.

The universe hums a silly tune,
As comets dance beneath the moon.
With every twist, the night gives way,
To laughter's thread that sways away.

In cosmic craft, no rules apply,
As punchlines spin and jokes soar high.
The night is young, the mischief grand,
In the seams of dreams, we take a stand.

Soft Gleams of the Night

The moon takes on a cheeky grin,
While owls debate where jokes begin.
With moonbeams flirting like a tease,
They whisper tales that bring us ease.

Stars giggle bright, twinkling loud,
As crickets sing their nightly crowd.
Each shimmer holds a secret jibe,
A cosmic laugh, an endless vibe.

A shadow slips, a cat's sly prance,
In twilight's waltz, we take our chance.
With laughter bubbling up like foam,
We roam the night, forever home.

In this soft glow, no worries strike,
The universe dons its jester's like.
Silly dreams weave through the air,
In midnight's arms, we dance and dare.

Gentle Hues of Dusk

As day dips low with clumsy grace,
The sun must wear a goofy face.
With pastels splashed against the sky,
It jokes that twilight is a sly guy.

Clouds dressed up in cotton spun,
Play hide and seek with rays that run.
A giggle rustles through the trees,
While shadows wiggle in the breeze.

The horizon wears a vibrant smile,
As night prepares its playful style.
Each hue a jest, each dusk a tease,
A canvas made for fun and ease.

We paint our dreams in colors bright,
As laughter twirls with fading light.
In gentle strokes, the day must fade,
So night can come out and invade.

Secrets in the Stillness

In quiet moments, giggles creep,
Where secrets hide and shadows leap.
The stillness buzzes with a jest,
As whispers tumble, never rest.

The night reveals its playful schemes,
With snickers caught in silken dreams.
Each pause a wink, each breath a laugh,
In stillness, joy is cut in half.

Crickets chirp a comic tune,
As stars play charades with the moon.
They share their tales in mystic light,
Unraveling laughs all through the night.

In serenity, mischief waits,
As night opens its funny gates.
So come and join this merry throng,
In secrets shared, where we belong.

Enigma of Starlit Textures

Under twinkling stars, I saw a sight,
A cat in a tutu, oh what a fright!
Dancing on rooftops, prancing with glee,
Chasing a shadow, as wild as can be.

Fluffy jumpers twirl in the breeze,
While squirrels are giggling, doing as they please.
Moonbeams tickle the edges of dreams,
As laughter erupts in glittering streams.

In the corner, a hedgehog in shades,
Flaunting his style, he never fades.
He trips and he tumbles, but still keeps his cool,
With a wink to the stars, he's nobody's fool.

The night wears a pattern, so silly, yet bright,
Like mismatched socks, a comedic delight.
With chaos and joy, the cosmos prepares,
For a whimsical dance in the fresh midnight airs.

The Beauty of Afterhours

When the clock strikes twelve, the mice start to sing,
While hats on the dog do a classy little fling.
Bees wear tuxedos, the ants have a ball,
In this strange nightlife, there's room for us all.

The moon, a giggler, peeks down from above,
At cats in their costumes, showing off love.
A party of owls, so dignified yet sly,
Debate the best fish and who gets the pie.

Tiny disco lights flash from a flower,
As insects groove in the midnight hour.
A beetle's the DJ, spinning tunes with flair,
While bugs on the dancefloor all clumsily pair.

And just as we thought it couldn't get better,
A frog leaps in dressed as an elegant debtor.
With croaks that resound, the fun multiplies,
In this glamorous chaos beneath the night skies!

Silken Echoes in Dusk

In twilight's mischief, the critters convene,
Bats tell tall tales, all silly and keen.
A raccoon in sequins, oh what a sight,
Attempting to juggle, oh what a fright!

Folks gather 'round with snacks on the grass,
As fireflies buzz in colorful class.
The frogs strike a pose on a lily pad high,
While crickets compose a sweet serenade nigh.

A turkey in shades struts down the lane,
Showing off moves that can't be explained.
Joined by a rooster, beatboxing with flair,
Who knew nighttime creatures could dance with such care?

As echoes of laughter resound ever so clear,
The night is a stage with its audience near.
With each funny moment, the world feels so bright,
In this joyous chaos of whimsical night.

Crystals on the Midnight Fabric

Under a canopy of whimsical dreams,
A snail dons a crown made of glittery beams.
Jiving on petals, he slides with delight,
As a squirrel in camo plays peek-a-boo right.

The stars wear pajamas, cozy and sweet,
While crabs on the sand engage in a beat.
Puppies in tutus prance all around,
Turning the forest to a playful playground.

Cupcakes are flying in frosted delight,
Landing on clouds, floating high in the night.
A pig in a jetpack zooms overhead,
Chasing a comet, while others turn red.

With giggles erupting, the moon cracks a smile,
As critters bond over chaos and style.
With crystals all twinkling, the night's never grim,
In this lively world, the fun's never slim.

Night's Silken Caress

In twilight's grip, the shadows prance,
A cat in heels begins to dance.
The stars above begin to chuckle,
As fireflies gather for a little huddle.

With every twirl, the moonlight's grin,
A moth in tux, where to begin?
He leaps and bounds, oh what a sight!
In fancy garb, he steals the night.

An owl who snores behind a tree,
Dreams of breadcrumbs dipped in brie.
While rabbits hop in polka dots,
Planning dances, tying knots.

The breeze gets playful, tickles the leaves,
As crickets join in with their witty heaves.
In this ball of whimsy, joy takes flight,
Where every creature bops with delight.

Starlit Veil of Secrets

Beneath the glow of stars so bright,
A squirrel juggles nuts by night.
He drops one down, it rolls away,
An acorn slip is quite the play!

The fireflies, in a playful fight,
Create a glow that's pure delight.
With twinkling butts, they shine and sway,
As laughter echoes, come what may.

Dancing shadows, a tree's slight bow,
They form a conga, take a bow.
Each leaf a hat, each branch a cane,
The night's a party, wild and insane!

A raccoon stumbles, clutching a pie,
Blame it on the stars up high.
With goofy moves, they cheer and shout,
In whispered secrets, we twist about.

Dusk's Woven Fantasies

At dusk, the fairy lights do bloom,
And shadows gather in every room.
The frogs are crooning in perfect tune,
While bathtubs fill with lavender moon.

A spider spinning tales so grand,
Weaves a web, but it's all out of hand.
The flies get caught — oh, what a plight!
Hoping for burgers before tonight.

The hedgehogs giggle, all snug in thread,
They prep a feast in a mushroom bed.
With tiny forks, they share a stew,
Of broccoli blended with berries too!

In every nook, the whispers fade,
From sly raccoons planning a parade.
A sprinkle of mischief, a dash of cheer,
Dusk's woven dreams are finally here!

A Dance of Nighttime Threads

The moon's a stage for critters grand,
Where ants and beetles form a band.
A tiny suit, a bowtie, how rare,
They waltz on dewdrops without a care.

A fox with flair performs a jig,
His tail's a twirl, it's quite the gig!
With every step, the stars align,
And disco lights from fireflies shine.

Each stitch of night wrapped up in play,
With chuckles echoing, come what may.
The grass blades sway, they tap their toes,
While squirrels shake it, striking poses.

In this carnival of furry delight,
They twine and reel into the night.
A party woven, dreams untold,
In every heartbeat, joy unfolds.

Ties that Bind in Darkness

In the dark, my shoelaces danced,
They tied themselves, oh what a chance!
A trip and stumble, laughter grew,
My feet were tangled, what to do?

The cat comes prancing, a playful tease,
She's judging me with such great ease.
With every step, a knot appears,
I'm just a jester, full of cheers!

The moonlight giggles, shining bright,
As my sneakers take off in flight.
I tumble and roll in a comic way,
A hiking trip? No! A circus play!

So here's to ties that bind at night,
They twist and twirl, such a sight!
With each stumble, I'll take my stand,
As a clumsy king, crown in hand!

Celestial Lacework

Stars above me, they shine and wink,
I reach for them, oh what a stink!
My arms go flailing, caught in dreams,
I'm weaving thoughts with silly schemes.

The Milky Way spills juice on my head,
I look like a cosmic pancake, oh dread!
With every stretch, I lose a shoe,
I wonder if penguins feel this too?

Galaxies blush as they see me slip,
Into the darkness, I take a dip.
But laughter bubbles under the stars,
Even my jammies are full of scars!

So dance beneath the heavens bright,
In mismatched socks, take a flight.
For in this silly cosmic game,
We're all the same; let's laugh and claim!

Fragments of a Midnight Reverie

In night's embrace, my thoughts take flight,
While snacks and giggles blend just right.
I ponder life, but much too loud,
As dreams of ice cream form a crowd.

A comet flies with a funky glide,
I wonder if it's ever tried
To eat spaghetti twirls, what a mess!
With sauce and stars, it aims to impress!

Midnight snacks lead to tangled feels,
I wear a hat made of peanut peels.
The fridge hums a whimsical tune,
As I sashay by, a chipmunk's boon!

So laugh with me in this dreamy haze,
And let our hearts do the crazy maze.
For every morsel in this cosmic spree,
Hides fragments of glee, just wait and see!

Nocturne in a Twirl of Silk

With a twirl, I find my way,
In silky chaos, where I stray.
The shadows giggle behind my back,
As I try to keep my snack on track.

A dance floor made of popcorn stars,
I stumble into cosmic guitars.
They strum a tune that sparks delight,
I'm twirling silly under moonlight!

With every step, the floorboards creak,
My feet resemble a drunken sneak.
The curtains laugh, they flap and sway,
As I giggle my way through the ballet!

In this nocturnal weave and spin,
Every pratfall feels like a win.
So grab a friend, and hold on tight,
For silly nights are pure delight!

Dance of the Silver Fabric

Twinkling threads in the night air,
Dancing lightly without a care.
A squirrel waltzes on the ground,
While a cat purrs, looking profound.

Glimmers giggle, the breeze takes flight,
Spinning tales till the morning light.
A hedgehog prances with little flair,
In the moon's glow, it sheds its stare.

Every tangle creates a jest,
Nature's party, a wild fest.
Laughter echoes, shadows sway,
As fabrics twirl and join the play.

And should you wander through this scene,
Expect the oddest sights to glean.
For with a chuckle, the night unfolds,
In silver whispers, magic molds.

Shadows Playing in Intricacy

A cat with shoes tiptoes near,
Beneath the stars, quite full of cheer.
Dancing shadows make their bed,
While the puzzled moon tilts its head.

In fabric folds, the rabbits scoff,
Looping loops that come and go off.
A wise old owl begins to sing,
As tangled threads feel just like spring.

Squirrels leap through the weaves and knots,
Beneath a sky that's been quite hot.
Each twinkling star, a wink or tease,
Driving onlookers to their knees.

If you listen closely for a while,
The night's shenanigans will make you smile.
For mysteries of fabric swirl,
In laughter's wake, the night will twirl.

Glistening Shadows of a Dream

When shadows giggle with delight,
Frogs wear hats, oh what a sight!
A zephyr whispers secrets rare,
While crickets croon without a care.

Glistening dreams on softest trails,
Even the moon creates funny tales.
A hedgehog steals a shine or two,
Sparking giggles in evening dew.

Each flickering star, a wink so sly,
The fireflies join in, oh my, oh my!
They dance like ribbons, all aglow,
In shadows' midst, their zeal will grow.

So if you wander beneath this dome,
Know laughter's where the wild things roam.
For dreams entwined in a giggling twist,
Create a night you can't resist.

Night's Fertile Softness

Under soft cover, mischief brews,
A hedgehog's hat made with cheetah hues.
With every step, he tries to prance,
Tickling the grass, he joins the dance.

The moon chuckles, lighting the way,
As creatures celebrate in a playful sway.
A bunny hops with an echoing squeal,
Wrappings of whispers, quite surreal.

Crickets plot and the owls conspire,
While fireflies flicker like stars on fire.
Woven giggles rise like mist,
In night's embrace, it's laughter's twist.

So join the fun, let worries fly,
For when night calls, do not be shy.
In fertile softness, chaos reigns,
As the world spins with joy unchains.

Shadows Dressed in Silver

Under the glow of a giggling moon,
Shadows twirl in a comical tune.
They dance on rooftops, they trip and they fall,
Like cats on a fence, they wobble and sprawl.

The clouds wear hats, embroidered with flair,
As bumbling stars juggle in midair.
A raccoon in a tux gives a wink and a nod,
As laughter erupts from a firefly squad.

The wise old owl hoots with a chuckle,
While squirrels show off in a nutty huddle.
With moonbeams as spotlights, the night takes the stage,
Where giggles and grins break free from their cage.

So let's toast to shadows, their slippery play,
In the silver-lit night, they'll merrily sway.
With mischief and glee, under skies oh so wide,
Laughter will sail on the moonlit tide.

Threads of Starlight

Threads of glitter spin tales in the air,
Of snickering comets with prankster flair.
A tapestry woven with laughter and jest,
As the universe giggles and nods in its vest.

Stars play hopscotch on bright moonbeams,
While fairies float by with mischievous dreams.
A unicorn stumbles, trips over a dream,
Causing starlight to scatter—oh, what a scene!

In these golden strands, surprises await,
Like a cat in a hat, they've tangled their fate.
With each twist and turn, they spark with delight,
In the webs spun by giggles of the night.

So come take a peek at this whimsical sight,
Where the threads of the cosmos are spun just right.
With each chuckle and shimmer, let joy take its flight,
As starlight and laughter weave together—so bright!

Midnight's Delicate Weave

At midnight, the moon plays with jests and with glee,
Weaving wonders as silly as can be.
With threads of laughter, the night fabric sings,
Of mischief and craziness, oh, what joy it brings!

Bouncing bunnies in jackets dance round with a spin,
While fireflies pop up, inviting us in.
The owls on their perches just roll their sly eyes,
At the antics unfolding beneath starry skies.

With a wink and a nod, the universe plays,
As shadows perform in their quirky displays.
Each twirl and each spin is a comedic delight,
In midnight's embrace, everything feels just right.

So let's bask in this glow, a night pure and free,
Where the laughter glistens like dew on a tree.
As we dance through the fabric, with whimsy we leave,
In the delicate weave of the night, we believe!

Ethereal Patterns Entwined

In a whimsical realm where the shadows can move,
Ethereal patterns create a grand groove.
With a wink of a comet and a jig from the stars,
They invite all the critters from near and from far.

The glowworms join in with rhythmic delight,
Their pulsing green lights adding zest to the night.
What fun it is, dancing out on the grass,
As the moon whispers secrets, a cosmic morass.

Caterpillars strut in their best frocks tonight,
Leading ladybugs under the celestial light.
They twirl and they spin, with elegance rare,
While giggling together in the cool midnight air.

So embrace all the laughter, let joy intertwine,
In the patterns of daisies, where moonbeams align.
With each chuckle and snicker adding spice to the tale,
These ethereal moments—we'll cherish and hail.

Dreaming in Midnight Hues

In shadows, found a sock, it winks,
With patterns that cause giggles and jinks.
A midnight snack of cheese and cake,
Who knew the fridge would start to quake?

The cat's on patrol, with curious eyes,
She thinks the moon's a giant prize.
With stealth, she pounces, misses the light,
And lands in a box, oh what a sight!

Undies on the ceiling, how'd they get there?
Perhaps a laundry fairy's antics, I swear!
As I sip tea from a silly cup,
Wondering whether I should clean up.

So under the stars, I conjure delight,
Who needs a plan? Let's take to flight!
In dreams, we dance, so freely we flit,
Laughing at life—oh, isn't it a hit?

Twilight's Tenuous Stitch

At dusk we stitch with thread so bright,
Fumbling fabric, oh what a sight!
The needle's a dance partner, awkward and shy,
Threaded with laughter, we both can fly.

Pumpkins are gossiping, whispering loud,
They spice up the evening, they're so proud.
One rolls away, startled by a breeze,
"Pumpkin Spice, take it easy, please!"

A spider spins tales of old and new,
While juggling my shoes, it really flew!
The night was young, with quirks to unfold,
Each moment a treasure, too funny to hold.

In starlit patches, a quilt with bright seams,
Laughter weaves memories, colorful dreams.
With every misstep, we twirl and slide,
In twilight's embrace, we shall not hide.

Veils of Celestial Light

A blanket of stars, with holes here and there,
A cosmic patchwork, full of flair.
Each twinkle's a wink, a playful tease,
As I sip my tea, it warms like cheese.

Aliens giggle as they float by,
"Is that your hair, or did it just die?"
With nebulae flashing like disco lights,
They turn bad dance moves into fun flights.

In the dance of the cosmos, I trip on a star,
"Watch out!" I shout, but they're near and far.
They laugh and they whirl, in a celestial ball,
While I'm just the clown, with hope to enthrall.

So under the gaze of the universe's grin,
We twirl and we tumble, let the night begin!
With laughter as stardust, we celebrate life,
In veils of delight, and not a hint of strife.

Soft Echoes in the Dark

Whispers at night, stir fry in my brain,
A waltz of the weird, a chuckle from pain.
As I chase soft echoes of giggles and glee,
Waking the shadows, they laugh back at me.

The fridge hums a tune, slightly off beat,
It's hosting a party, where's all the meat?
As I dance through the room, like a hippo in flight,
Orbited by snacks, what a ridiculous sight!

The curtains are swirling, just like my thoughts,
With every misstep, I forget what I bought.
So many cushions, an obstacle course,
I tumble and giggle, can't change my course.

When darkness speaks softly, it finds you in glee,
Turning mundane to magic, endlessly free.
With laughter as our guide, we stumble and play,
In soft echoes of night, we toss gloom away.

Dark Whispers in Fluttering Threads

A spider's dance with nimble feet,
Whirls of humor, oh so sweet.
Catcher of dreams on a silken path,
Tickling the night's gentle laugh.

Twinkling stars, a winking crew,
Wobbling worms, they join the view.
Giggling grins beneath the glow,
Spinning tales of joy and woe.

Breezes whisper, secrets tease,
While moths play tag with the trees.
Tripping along the chilly air,
With giggles echoing everywhere.

In the dark, a jester hides,
Foolish shadows take great strides.
With every flitter and fluttering sound,
Laughter dances all around.

Patterns of Enchantment Underneath

Underneath the sparkling hue,
Little critters share a brew.
A cup of giggles, a dash of cheer,
While shadows shimmy, far and near.

In the garden, jokes are spun,
Bumblebees buzz just for fun.
Rustling leaves giggle soft,
Whispers of the fairy loft.

At midnight's hour, a playful twist,
Winks from twinkling stars persist.
Rabbits chuckle, owls roll eyes,
As the world in laughter lies.

With a wink, the shadows prance,
Joining in the merry dance.
A tapestry of joy displayed,
In patterns that the night has made.

Night's Mysterious Emblems

Under stars, the stories fling,
Whispers caught on a moonlit string.
Silly giggles filling the air,
As shadows play without a care.

A flock of owls hoots in jest,
While the crickets host a fest.
The porch light flickers, flicks of fate,
As every critter starts to wait.

With giggly shadows at our side,
We chase the night, but never hide.
Frogs in tuxedos jump around,
While the wind joins in with a sound.

In the mist, the glee unravels,
As puzzle pieces dance in travels.
With every chuckle, dimples gleam,
In night's embrace, we laugh and dream.

Threads of Celestial Whisper

Whispers tangled in the breeze,
Twinkling stars, they tease with ease.
In a garden of giggles, shadows play,
While the moonlight joins, hip-hip-hooray!

Wiggly worms sport tiny shoes,
Breaking rules, they love to snooze.
As fireflies blink their tiny lights,
They join the fun and playful fights.

Frisky breezes play peek-a-boo,
While the night conjures something new.
A chorus of chuckles fills the air,
With dancing thoughts, we just don't care.

In the realm of funny schemes,
All the world's whirling in dreams.
With threads woven tight in delight,
We frolic in the joy of night.

Serenade of the Hidden Patterns

In shadows dance, the threads unwind,
A cat in heels, so poorly aligned.
With swirls and loops, the fabric spins,
A jester's cap, where the laughter begins.

The owls wear glasses, the squirrels in hats,
While snoring toads play cards with the bats.
A patchwork quilt of giggles abound,
Where silly secrets in stitches are found.

The moon plays tricks, with a wink and a nod,
An umbrella hides where the frogs had a prod.
The stars twinkle chuckles, in bright little dots,
As fairies do pirouettes wearing polka spots.

So laugh with the night, let your worries flee,
These whimsical patterns are wild and free.
Where every creak and rustle ignites,
A serenade spun from the quirkiest nights.

Nightfall's Couture of Wonder

A gown made of giggles, the night wears with pride,
Spinning tales of mice, on a magical ride.
With pockets of sunshine and buttons of cheer,
Every shadow is cast with a curious leer.

The moon, a designer, with fabrics so bright,
Frogs critique fashion in the cool of the night.
Twinkling birds, in their feathered attire,
Fashion shows where the owls never tire.

Pillow fights break out in the cool gentle breeze,
As sparkly stitches float down from the trees.
Crickets serve drinks in their best dress coats,
Toasting to silliness on their tiny boats.

With laughter aplenty, the stars play their part,
As nightfall's couture warms the ticklish heart.
In the embrace of whimsy that wraps us tight,
The runway of dreams shines brightly tonight.

Secrets of the Gentle Night

Whispers of mischief glide through the gloom,
While shadows reveal a grand feast in the room.
Dancing with fireflies, parties ignite,
Where even the flowers seem giggly and light.

A gopher in slippers serves chaotically fun,
While raccoons juggle under the sweet silver sun.
The owls exchange secrets, mischievous glints,
In this cozy confetti of curious hints.

The moon sneezes softly, a chuckle escapes,
As hiccupping hedgehogs concoct silly capes.
Polka dot shadows leap with delight,
In the gentle embrace of the softening night.

So let your heart giggle, let your spirit roam,
In this dreamlit adventure, you've found your home.
With the secrets of night twirling all around,
Laughter and joy in every nook found.

Moonlit Threads of Fantasy

The moon weaves dreams with shimmering strands,
While socks play hopscotch, forming silly bands.
Stars twirl through galaxies, giggling in flight,
In a fashion parade of the joyful night.

Dandelions giggle as gusts blow a tune,
While penguins on ice sip sweet lemonade moons.
A patch of wild berries dips low in transformation,
With tiny fingers crafting wild celebration.

With zany adventures where whimsy prevails,
The crickets compose the most outlandish tales.
A bear in a bowtie serves waffles and fluff,
Inviting us all to laugh, dance, and bluff.

So sway with the fabric that flutters and sways,
In the glow of the night, where all laughter plays.
With threads of pure joy that entwine each heart,
In this moonlit fantasy, creativity starts.

Nocturnal Threads of Enchantment

A cat in a hat, with a twinkle in eye,
Pretends he's a wizard, making clouds fly.
With threads from the sky, he stitches a grin,
As owls hold their breath, hoping to win.

A squirrel named Larry rolls dice on a moss,
Dreaming of treasures that bloom like a boss.
He laughs at the moon, plays poker with stars,
While frogs sing his praises from nearby guitars.

The trees have a sway, with a shimmy and shake,
While fireflies giggle, their lights start to quake.
The breeze whispers jokes, in a soft, playful tone,
As night throws a party, and no one's alone.

So pull up a chair, join the fun and the fest,
Under nighttime's blanket, we'll dance with the best.
With threads made of starlight, we'll stitch up delight,
In this magical moment, so blissful and bright.

Moonlit Embroidery of Stars

A moonbeam's a noodle, slippery and long,
It twirls like spaghetti, where shadows belong.
With crickets composing a chorus so fine,
We dine on the laughter that sparkles like wine.

The tulips are giggling, their petals a-flutter,
While hedgehogs in tuxes break bread with a mutter.
They sip from the puddles, laughing all night,
In this quirky banquet, the stars shine so bright.

A raccoon serves punch with a dash of moon dust,
He flips like a pro, in this raucous, wild thrust.
The owls do the limbo, the night owls can't get,
Enough of this revel, oh what a vignette!

So let's toast to the twilight, the weirdness to share,
With friendships and fun, and no signs of a care.
For in this grand tapestry, laughter's the key,
As night stitches moments, like magic, carefree.

Dreams Woven in Twilight's Embrace

Twilight wraps softly, a blanket of hue,
As rabbits play hopscotch with dreams that come true.
A skunk spins around, with a flair so divine,
While fireflies giggle, they join in the line.

The stars start their stitching, a crooked little seam,
While rabbits serve cookies, just part of the dream.
With a twirl and a whirl, they dance through the night,
Creating a party, a whimsical sight.

A hedgehog in sneakers, doing cartwheels with flair,
Bids everyone welcome, "There's snacks if you dare!"
The trees hold their breath, as the owls take a bow,
This kingdom of fun, oh, where laughter can grow.

So let's twiddle our thumbs, and spin tales full of cheer,
In this soft twilight, let's banish all fear.
For dreams woven gently, with laughter so bright,
In the heart of the darkness, we'll dance until light.

The Fabric of Night's Reverie

In the fabric of night, threads jitter and hum,
Where raccoons wear vests, and the owls go 'yum!'
There's a party for shadows, all creatures of whim,
With a jive and a jig, they delight in the dim.

A fox plays the piano, it's jazzy and bold,
While moths do the tango, their wings decorated gold.
With a swish and a flick, they spin round and round,
In this festival of folly, where joy knows no bound.

The moon shares its secrets, with a wink and a grin,
As night wears a crown that is feathered and thin.
The stars lend their sparkle to the dance on the floor,
While laughter erupts, like a popcorn encore.

So gather around, let the fun times begin,
In this whimsical wonder, there's no way to thin.
For in this enactment of skies dark and deep,
We stitch up the moments, in memories to keep.

www.ingramcontent.com/pod-product-compliance
Lightning Source LLC
Chambersburg PA
CBHW070311120526
44590CB00017B/2634